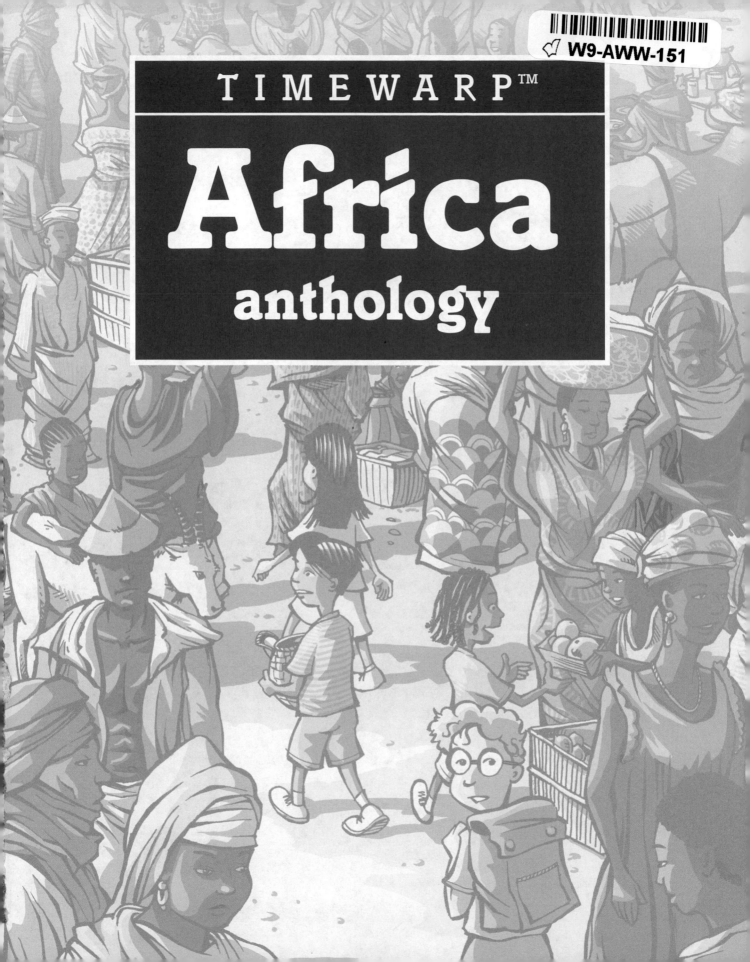

TABLE OF CONTENTS

O AFRICA

O Africa,
Who do men say that you are?
Having risen out of the mists of earliest time,
A land of mystery and legend
With many secrets yet to be revealed—
Revelations of vanished peoples and lost kingdoms,
You once were called the "dark continent."

O Africa,
Thought to be the birthplace of mankind,
You taught us to mold and make the earth into our home.
Shaping languages and lives, feeding other lands,
You became a mother of great nations,
An artist painting in shades of copper-brown and black.
Some have called you "the motherland."

O Africa,
Rising and falling throughout history
Like the sand dunes of your great deserts,
Stretching endlessly
Like the open plains that are your savannas,
Yielding many treasures from jungle growth and soil,
You've given far more to the world than you've taken.

O Africa,
Where have you come to now?
Are you the land that some show you to be?
Will you be forever trapped behind real and imagined bars of
    poverty and war?
Or will you burst forth and remind the world of your glorious past?
Will you remind us that you are, after all, one of the seven?
O Africa,
What will you become?

INTO AFRICA

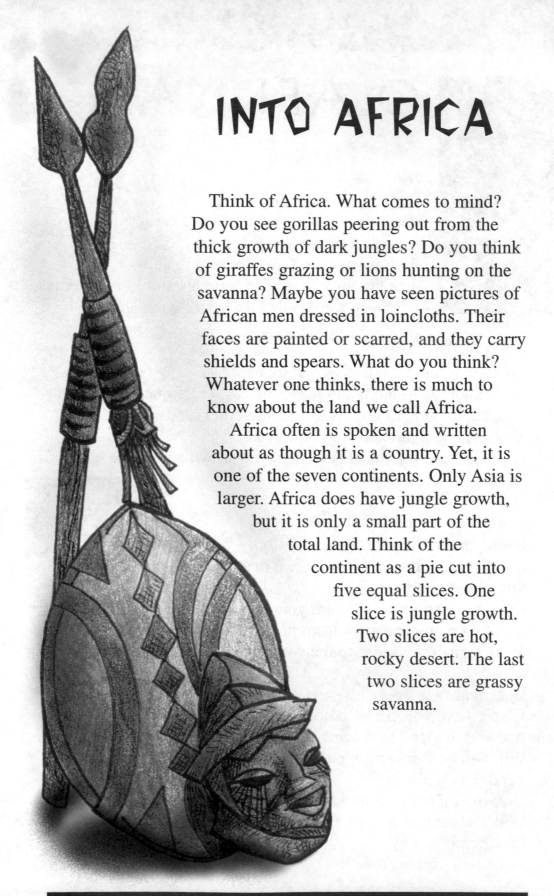

Think of Africa. What comes to mind?
Do you see gorillas peering out from the
thick growth of dark jungles? Do you think
of giraffes grazing or lions hunting on the
savanna? Maybe you have seen pictures of
African men dressed in loincloths. Their
faces are painted or scarred, and they carry
shields and spears. What do you think?
Whatever one thinks, there is much to
know about the land we call Africa.

Africa often is spoken and written
about as though it is a country. Yet, it is
one of the seven continents. Only Asia is
larger. Africa does have jungle growth,
but it is only a small part of the
total land. Think of the
continent as a pie cut into
five equal slices. One
slice is jungle growth.
Two slices are hot,
rocky desert. The last
two slices are grassy
savanna.

MALI

SONG HAY

ASHANTI

BENIN

KUSH

AXUM

MEROE

AFRICA

GREAT ZIMBABWE

MADAGASCAR

Africa is home to some of the greatest natural sites in the world. The word *Sahara* means desert. It also names the largest desert in the world. The Sahara covers most of northern Africa. The area was green with plants thousands of years ago. The soil was rich. The Nile River is the longest river in the world. It begins at Lake Victoria, one of the great lakes of the world. It flows north to the Mediterranean Sea.

The people of Africa live in many different ways. Some live in bustling cities. Some live in small villages. Some share the wilderness areas with animals. Others live in or near the deserts.

There are more than 50 countries in Africa. There are more

than 730 million people. Most are black Africans. They live in almost 800 groups. The groups are not all the same. They do not look the same. They do not live the same. They do not think alike.

Today, Africa is a land in turmoil. That means a lot of the people are struggling. Some live well. Many do not. The same is true for countless other places in the world. Has this always been true for Africa? What was life like on the continent long ago?

For a long time, very little was known about Africa's ancient history. Researchers have begun to try to learn more. They have begun to share their findings. What they have learned is shedding new light on the continent. What was once unclear is now made plain. As we learn more about it, Africa is being reborn.

We know that Africa was once a land of great kingdoms. From them, much of the rest of the world grew and prospered. A number of the ideas by which people live today came from the kingdoms of ancient Africa. The first of these sprang from the eastern part of the continent. The area was called Nubia. The kingdoms were Kush, Meroë, and Axum. Next were the kingdoms of the west. They were Ghana, Mali, Songhai, and Benin. Great Zimbabwe followed in the south. The last of the great kingdoms was fairly modern. It was called Ashanti.

The kingdoms represented times when Africa was at its best. Knowledge and gains made during these times carried over to other places. They made life better for Africans. They made life better for other people in the world, too.

Kingdoms of the Nile

The great Nile River flows north through Africa. It flows for more than 4,000 miles. It gives life to people along its banks. It has done so for thousands of years. It watered the earliest of the great kingdoms of Africa.

Nubia

Long ago, the Nile flowed through a part of Africa known as Nubia. It was an area that is now part of the Sahara, but it was not hot and dry then. It was green and fertile.

Nubia was one of the oldest African cultures. It was very wealthy. It began around 3800 B.C. It quickly became a main source of traded goods. Many natural resources were found there. The people dug gold from the land. They also harvested a kind of wood. It was called ebony. They had many cattle. Ostrich plumes were traded. Ivory from the tusks of elephants was too. Both were used to make goods for kings and queens.

The Nubians made good use of their fertile land. The farming methods they used gave good crops. They raised strong cattle and other livestock.

Some researchers believe the ancient Nubians were some of the first humans on Earth. They can be traced to earlier times than most other groups of people. The findings show they were highly civilized. They had laws. They had rules for behaving and living together.

After some time, Nubia had a neighbor to the north. It was Egypt. The two cultures traded goods. They traded ideas. They fought, too. At times, Nubia was under the rule of Egypt. Kush was the name Egypt used for Nubia. The name held until the area and its kingdoms were completely taken over for the last time. That was in the year 350 A.D.

Little else is known about the people of early Nubia. Over time, the Sahara began to dry up. The people then moved farther south, away from Egypt. They built a new kingdom. They kept the name Egypt had given them. They called the new kingdom Kush. It later would rise to become one of the great African kingdoms.

Egypt

Egypt was the best known of the ancient African kingdoms. It was on the Nile River north of Nubia. It was very powerful because of where it was.

The Nile was called the "lifeblood of Egypt." The people used the river to trade. They traded incense, grain, and other goods for gold. Nubia was one trading partner. Later, they traded with the new kingdom of Kush. The Nile made crops grow. Its yearly flood made the soil rich. The Egyptians wanted to know when the floods might come. They studied the sun, moon, and stars. From what they learned, they made the world's first known 12-month calendar. It had 365 days.

Eat, Drink, Speak

Hound, Dog

Army, Soldier

See

Build

Drive away

The ancient Egyptians created a style of writing. It was around 3000 B.C. It was called hieroglyphs. It used symbols and pictures. This let them record history. It helped them share knowledge.

The rulers of Egypt became known all over the world. They were called pharaohs. The people built great tombs for them. Some were inside pyramids. Did the idea come from their Nubian neighbors? Some researchers thought so. Tomb paintings told about the lives and customs of the ancient Egyptians. They revealed many things, but much is still to be learned.

In Egyptian families, fathers were in charge of money. Mothers cared for the home and children. Children spent much of their time learning adult skills. They worked in the fields. They did chores. Male children often became apprentices to their fathers. They learned to do what their fathers did. Children from rich families sometimes went to school to become writers. Some became army officers.

Egyptians cared about how they looked. They liked to be clean. Clues to what they used for makeup and cleanliness have been found in tombs. Other clues were in tomb paintings. Oils and creams protected them from hot sun and dry winds. Eye paint was the most common makeup.

Both men and women wore jewelry. They wore earrings, bracelets, and anklets. They wore rings and beaded necklaces. Many wore good-luck charms called amulets.

The kingdom of Egypt lasted longer than any in history. Its states were formed by 3500 B.C. At one time, Egypt controlled the northern part of Nubia. Ideas and ways of living were exchanged. Some were blended. Later, southern Nubia took over part of Egypt. This happened around 750 B.C. They ruled for about 100 years. Then, other invaders challenged them. Egypt was left to the Assyrians.

Kush

The Kushites moved their capital farther south after Egypt was taken. The new one was Meroë. It was very powerful.

The natural resources were like those in northern Nubia. They found gold and other minerals. There were different kinds of wood, gum, and ivory. Local ore was mined. It was made into iron. It is thought that people in many places learned to work iron from the people of Meroë.

Buildings and art in Kush were like those of Egypt. Some things were different. Kushites added ideas. The pyramids were smaller. They were steeper. The people built temples and palaces. They were filled with pottery. Some pottery pictured hunters and animals. Some showed plants and flowers. There

were carvings of rulers. They were shown with fantastic jewelry. Other carvings were of lions and elephants. Both animals were important to the Kushites. Elephants were used in wars.

The language of Meroë is a mystery. It is very much like Egypt's. Many symbols are undefined. Progress has been made, but much is left to learn. Studying the language will help researchers learn more about Kush.

We know far less about Nubia or Kush than we know of Egypt. Why is this so? Many have asked the question. A great number of people think the key to the answer is the Nile River.

In 1971, the Aswan High Dam was finished. It was built across the Nile. It is 375 feet tall and 11,811 feet long. It stands where the river ran through Nubia. It caused a lake to form. The lake is Lake Nasser.

The water from the lake brought electric power for nearby people. It caused problems as well. As the dam was built, those who lived nearby had to move. They left their ancient lands. Their culture and language were uprooted. Researchers saved many artifacts. They moved graveyards and temples. They moved what was left of settlements. They moved as much as they could. Still, much of ancient Nubia was buried underwater in Lake Nasser.

Ra and Hathor

Many years ago, there lived a great ruler named Ra. His was a splendid kingdom. The kingdom thrived, and men followed Ra's rules. They greatly respected him for many years.

As time passed, Ra grew old. The people in his kingdom began to ignore his rules. Some even made fun of him. This made him very angry. He called on the elders of his council for help.

They held a secret meeting. All of the council members listened carefully as Ra spoke. He told all that was happening. His father was one of the elders on the council. His father's name was Nu.

Ra said to his father, "You are the oldest of the council, and I am your son. I seek your advice. The men of my kingdom speak badly of me. They make fun of me. I am very angry. I am so angry I want to be rid of them. But, I do not think doing away with them now is wise. What advice do you have for me?"

Nu thought for a long time before he answered. "You are a great ruler, Ra. You are even stronger than I was. You only need to banish those who speak badly about you from the kingdom. The others will know that you are still a great ruler. They will respect you again."

Ra did as his father advised. He banished the men from his kingdom. The men were taken across the Nile and told never to return. All was well in the kingdom, but this didn't last for long.

The men in the kingdom wanted a new ruler. They began to look for another man to be in charge. They planned to banish Ra from the kingdom.

Ra met with the elders of his council a second time. They advised him to take a stronger stand. He would have to do something more severe than banishing people from the kingdom. "The people in this kingdom have too much free time," one of the elders said. "If they had to work harder, they would have no time to plot against you, Ra."

The rest of the council agreed. So, Ra began to look for an overseer. He needed someone to take charge of the workers. He wanted someone to make sure they worked many hard hours. They would not have time to make plans against him.

Ra found a woman named Hathor. She was a warrior. Hathor was stronger than any man in the kingdom. She struck fear into the hearts of all men, women, and children. Ra told her what he wanted her to do. She respected Ra and wanted to help him.

Hathor hired men to be in charge of getting all the people in the kingdom to work in the morning. She made sure that all villagers were up by sunrise each morning to exercise. They had to be at work an hour later. Every worker was allowed a short break at mid-morning and a slightly longer break for the midday meal. Then, they had to go back to work. The people worked until just before dark. They then were sent home for dinner and sleep. Each day started and ended the same way.

Hathor's men were also in charge of making sure that everyone in their group was working as hard as possible. There was no room for slacking. Sick workers saw only the doctors that Hathor allowed. If Hathor agreed, the workers spent the day in the hospital. As soon as they were released, they went back to work.

Ra was pleased with the results. He was most pleased with the fact that no one had time to make plans against him. The people were too busy or too tired to even think about him. Things went more smoothly than he had planned. He was very happy. The people produced so many new products that Ra began to trade with other kingdoms. There was a great demand for what his people made. They shipped more and more as the time passed. Ra paid Hathor a bonus each time a shipment was sent.

Hathor had a greedy heart. She became even greedier as time passed. She wanted more money and power. Hathor began to work the people longer hours. They had fewer breaks. She expected more and more of them. She took away their meal times. They were not even allowed to break for water. The workers began to get sick. Some died. Still, Hathor wanted more. She had to have more money and more power. Finally one day, she decided that she could run the kingdom better than Ra. She began to plan his overthrow. She intended to take over the whole kingdom.

One of Hathor's men did not like what was happening to the workers. "This cannot continue," he said. "Hathor must be stopped." He went to Ra's palace. He told Ra how Hathor was treating the people. Ra listened to the man, but he wanted to see for himself.

Ra visited the villages. He found the same things in each one. People were sick. They were weak from hunger and thirst. Some were dying. Ra knew he had to stop Hathor. Events were not happening as he had intended. He only wanted the people to work enough to keep them from making plans against him. He did not want them to die.

Ra knew that Hathor was too powerful for him. He would be unable to defeat her by force. He met with his council in another secret meeting. They devised a plan. They would get Hathor out of the kingdom.

Ra called his cook into his inner throne room. "Close the door," Ra said. "You must mix a special drink. It must be very tasty. It must be so tasty that Hathor cannot resist drinking it."

The cook went to work. In a few days, he had created a wonderful beverage for Ra. The council met again. They tested the drink. All agreed that it was the best they had ever tasted. The real test was yet to come.

Ra called Hathor into his throne room. She was very excited because she was expecting another bonus. He had a meal prepared for them. He also invited the council to attend.

After Hathor greeted the council, they sat down to dinner. Understanding Hathor's desire for fame and power, Ra announced a surprise for her. He said the cook had created a special drink in her honor. It was to be named whatever Hathor called it. It would become the only drink allowed in the kingdom. "No one will drink from his cup until Hathor has named the drink," he declared.

Hathor was thrilled with the news. She quickly emptied her cup. "This is wonderful!" she exclaimed. "I will have to have another cup before I decide what to call it." She drank a second cup. She still could not settle on a name.

The council sat quietly watching and waiting. They knew that her drink had a special ingredient added to it. The cook had put a root in the drink. It would make Hathor fall asleep. The root had no flavor, but it was very powerful. They waited, and the drink soon took effect on Hathor. She slumped over onto the table. She began to snore.

When they were sure she was sound asleep, Ra called his royal army. They took Hathor in a boat out to the middle of the Mediterranean Sea. She slept during the trip. They sailed for 10 days. They found an island. They left Hathor there and returned to the kingdom.

Hathor awakened to find herself on the desolate island. She had no food. She had no fresh water. No one else lived on the island. She was alone. She had been stranded with no way to get off the island.

Back at the kingdom, Ra and the people had a great party to celebrate. Hathor was gone for good. Ra released the people from the strict working hours that Hathor had set for them. The people remembered and felt ashamed of what they had done. They regretted plotting against Ra. He always had been a fair and just ruler. He still was. He lived happily and enjoyed their respect for the rest of his days.

THE LEGEND OF THE WAX CROCODILE

The following story is an adaptation of an African legend of the same name. It comes from ancient Egypt. It is one of several stories of magic the sons of Pharaoh Khufu told their father.

A pharaoh once went on a long trip. As was the custom in that day, he did not walk alone. His counselors and servants went with him. They stopped at the village of a well-known scribe along the way. The scribe invited them to stay at his home to rest. Their animals could have a break from the long journey. The scribe lived in a large home. There was plenty of room for the pharaoh and his men.

Behind the house was a large garden. The scribe's wife liked to spend time in the garden. It had several places for her to sit. She could enjoy its beauty. It had fountains and ponds. They added to the beauty.

One evening as she sat in the garden, one of the pharaoh's servants walked into her private sitting place. He did not mean to do so. It was an accident. Each thought no one else was there. They startled one another.

"What are you doing in my garden?" the scribe's wife asked.

"Oh, I am terribly sorry," answered the young man. "I didn't know you were here. I just wanted to see this garden. I will leave right away."

The wife knew he was one of the pharaoh's servants and asked him to stay. A plan formed in her mind. She liked shiny, sparkly things. She collected them. She knew the pharaoh carried gold and many different jewels with him. She wanted the gold and other jewels. She hoped to talk the young man into helping her get them.

The scribe's wife talked with the young man for a long time. The more they talked, the more comfortable he became with her. He spoke of his family and friends. He spoke of his job in the pharaoh's house. She learned that he was upset with the pharaoh. He did not like the way the pharaoh treated servants. The scribe's wife was quite pleased to hear this bit of news. She thought it would be useful. It was getting late. She advised the man to go back to the house. They would meet again in the garden the next day.

They met to talk the next afternoon as agreed. They talked for many hours. The young man became even more relaxed with the scribe's wife. That was part of her plan. It was almost time to tell him what she had in mind. She decided to do so the next day.

The next afternoon, they met in their usual place in the garden. Unknown to either of them, the scribe's servant followed them to the garden. He hid behind one of the plants to find out what was happening. He listened as the scribe's wife told her young friend of her desire for the pharaoh's jewels and gold. They talked and made plans until after dark. Then, they left the garden, each going their separate way.

The scribe's servant waited until they left the garden. He went back to the house. Then, he met with the scribe and told him all that he had heard.

"So, they plan to steal from the pharaoh," said the scribe. "I cannot allow that to happen in my home. We must stop them." He took his servant into an inner room and removed a magic box from a shelf. "Follow the young man to the lake in the morning. Throw what is in this box into the lake as he bathes," he said to the servant. The servant took the box. He went to his room, promising to do as he had been told.

The next morning, the pharaoh's servant went to the lake to bathe. The scribe's servant followed. He stood on the shore of the lake behind the young man. He opened the box. It held a small wax crocodile. There was also a note. It read, "Tell me what you want me to do. I will do the job for you."

"Rid the pharaoh of his unfaithful servant. Take him away beneath the waters of the lake," the man said. He threw the crocodile into the lake.

The moment the crocodile hit the water, it came to life and swam straight for the bathing servant. It snatched the young man under the water's surface. The crocodile took him to the Underworld beneath the waters of the lake.

That evening, the pharaoh looked for his servant. He asked all his people to search for him. No one could find the servant. The pharaoh went to the scribe. He asked the scribe to help him find his lost servant.

"Oh, Pharaoh, waste not your time on the servant. He was unfaithful to you, as was my wife. Together, they planned to steal your treasures. My wife desired the gold and jewels you carry. She and the servant plotted to take them," confessed the scribe. Then, he told the pharaoh what had happened to the young man.

"You have dealt well with my servant," said the pharaoh. "But, your work is not done. I command that your wife shares his fate. If she wants to plot against me, her pharaoh, let her do so in the Underworld with her friend."

The scribe brought his wife to the pharaoh. She was accused of her crime and sentenced to be thrown into the lake. The crocodile waited just below the surface of the water. It seized the woman and took her to the Underworld. The woman, the servant, and the crocodile never were heard from again.

The Drum

Drumbeats sound in the village square.
Dembe hears. He must go there.
"Come, Mother, take me where the drummers play.
I must go and learn, for I will drum one day."

"No, sweet Dembe, the drumming will keep.
It is time for a nap. You must lie down and sleep.
Heed my words, Dembe, and you will see.
You will beat the drum as was meant to be.

"For when your time to go does come,
I will give to you a most wonderful drum.
You'll drum the rhythms of days long past,
The heartbeats of great ones who sleep at last.

"You will drum of birth. You will drum of life.
You will drum of joy, happiness, and strife.
You'll give the people another voice.
You'll speak for them as they mourn and rejoice.

"Then, when darkest night falls, and you can drum no more,
You'll close your eyes and drift to that distant shore.
Your drum and the stories it tells will remain,
For someone new to come and tell them again.

"Then, you'll be reborn, Dembe, in this drum song.
It will sound out loud and deep and strong.
You'll live for many generations to come.
Yes, you'll live forever in the beat of the drum."

WEST AFRICAN KINGDOMS

The kingdoms of West Africa were widely known. They sprang up near the Niger River long ago. The land on which they stood was rich with gold. It was rich for growing crops, too.

These kingdoms constantly fought for control of land. They fought over gold. Kingdoms rose and fell in a matter of a few years. Things were always changing. People and cultures changed. The end of the gold trade marked the end of the West African kingdoms.

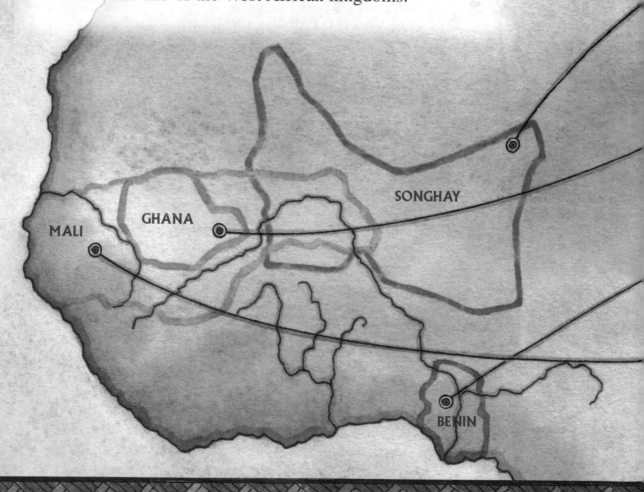

MALI

GHANA

SONGHAY

BENIN

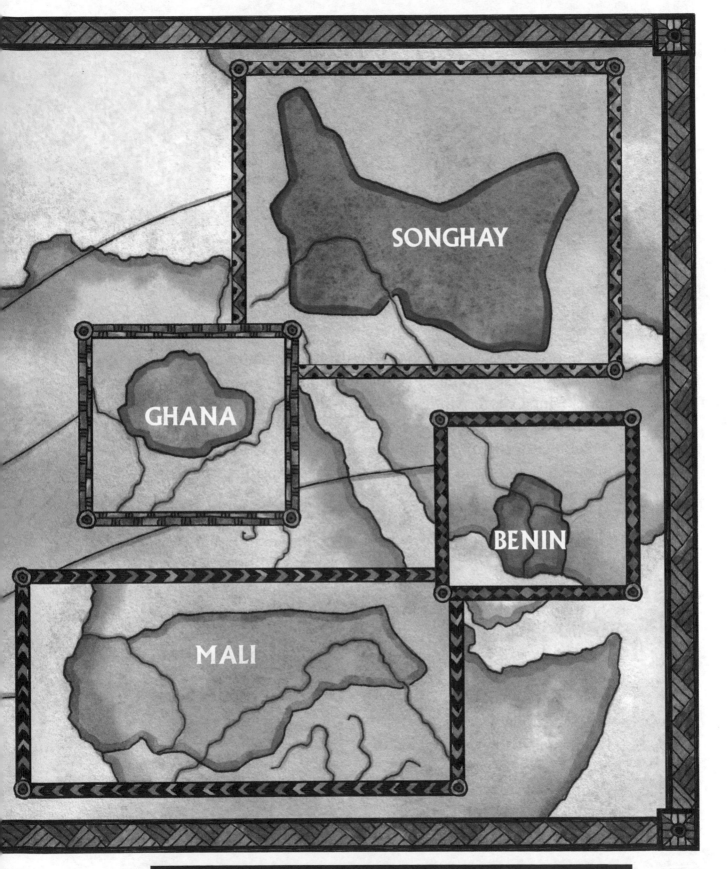

SONGHAY

GHANA

BENIN

MALI

Ghana

Today, Ghana is in southwest Africa. It is on the coast. It is 400 miles from an ancient kingdom. The kingdom also was called Ghana.

No one knows when the kingdom came into being. Some think the Soninke people came together under a great leader. He was Dinga Cisse. Stories about him differ. All call him an outsider. He was from far away.

Much that we know about Ghana came from writings. Some came from traders, travelers, and historians. Most had been there to trade or visit.

Ghana was a large kingdom in 1000 A.D. It widened its borders by taking over nearby lands. The kingdom lasted 1,000 years.

The people were warlike. They overtook many kingdoms. They were also master craftsmen. Some made iron tools or weapons. Others made jewelry. They used gold, silver, and copper. They made sandals, pottery, and cloth. Many items were traded.

Ghana was called "The Land of Gold." Trade grew when people began to use camels to carry gold. Ghana became powerful. Its people became rich.

Wealth mainly came by trading. They traded with Arabs. The Arabs crossed the Sahara to trade. It took two months by camel. When they got there, they pounded large drums. They left their goods and walked away from them. The villagers came with their goods. They left them beside the Arabs' goods and went back to the village. If the Arabs liked what was left, they beat the drums again. This let the villagers know the trade was good. The Arabs picked up the goods and left for home.

Ghana fell to outsiders who wanted to control the gold. The land was abused. Many outsiders had herds. The livestock ate many plants. With more farming, the soil became poor. It was hard to grow food for the people and for trade. A group called Soso finally claimed the kingdom's center. The Ghana kingdom ended.

Mali

The Soso began to move against another group. It was the Mandingo. Their leader was Sundiata. He convinced the Mandingo to fight. They took Ghana from the Soso.

Sundiata made the kingdom smaller. It became part of Mali. This was in the 1200s. The kingdom of Mali lasted 300 years.

Gold was important in many African kingdoms. This was true for Mali. It was a main trade item, but it was not the only one. Mali also traded salt and copper. Gold dust and crops were traded as well.

Timbuktu was in Mali. It was a trade center on the Niger River for many years. Caravans passed through it. The area brought more riches to the kingdom.

Mansa Musa was the best-known leader of Mali. He made a famous trip. It was to Mecca. He admired the buildings there. Mud bricks and wood beams were used. They made strong buildings. Two stories, upper and lower, could be made. Mansa Musa had his people copy the method of building.

Mansa Musa was very rich. Writers say he carried a ton of gold with him on his Mecca trip. It weighed 2,000 pounds. He took hundreds of maids and slaves. It was said the slaves had golden staffs.

Mansa Musa's trip added to history in another way. He brought back writers. They wrote about his rule. They only worked for him. Reading and writing did not spread to the people.

After he died, many other kings took turns on the throne. Some were strong. Many were weak. Mali was known to be peaceful. Weak rulers made it an easy target. Its neighbors attacked. This led to its end in 1500.

Songhay

Songhay grew into an empire when Mansa Musa died. He had been the ruler of Mali. Songhay became the most powerful kingdom in West Africa. Its rise began under Sunni Ali.

Sunni Ali had a great military. It was made of a fleet of ships. His men were highly trained. His fleet took over Timbuktu and other lands. The Berbers were invaders. They had destroyed other kingdoms. But, the Songhay Empire pushed them away as it grew north.

Sunni Ali led Songhay for 27 years. Muhammad Touré followed him. He wanted to increase the kingdom. He took over more lands. The government was reorganized. He brought people from different lands together under his rule.

Touré thought that people should use the same weights, measures, and money in trading. This helped to bring the different groups of people together also. It is what helped Songhay to become the largest empire in African history.

Songhay had civil war in the end. The people fought one another. The land dried up. Many people became ill.

A new group came from North Africa in 1591. They were Moroccans. The Songhay army and navy were strong, but they were defeated. They fought with spears, swords, and bows and arrows. These things were no match for the Moroccans' guns.

Benin

Benin was south of Songhay. It was founded in the 1200s. No one is sure how the culture began.

The people of Benin made many things from bronze. They made objects from copper, too. Some bronze plates hung on the walls of the oba's, or king's, palace. Shapes of heads were common. Jewelry was made from gold and ivory.

The metal craftsmen had their own ways of making the heads and other shapes. It was called the lost wax method. It took three or four hours from start to finish.

First, a model was made of wax. Then, a mold of clay was formed around the wax model. This was left to harden. Once it did, the whole thing was heated. The wax melted away. It left a hollow space in the shape of the model. Molten metal was poured into the hollow. It cooled and hardened. Last, the mold was broken. The statue was ready.

Like many other kingdoms, the people traded with outsiders. They traded spices and ivory with Europeans. They traded slaves.

One trade partner was Portugal, a country in Europe. The Portuguese first thought trading with Benin would be easy. Benin traders were very shrewd. They were skilled at dealing. The two groups were friendly for a time. Then, Portugal wanted more slaves than Benin could give. Benin wanted guns. Portugal would not give them guns. Matters became worse. For 200 years, Benin clashed with other trade partners as well.

Another partner was Britain. In the late 1800s, the British wanted to control some of the trade that belonged to Benin. They wanted to force Benin to trade as they wanted them to. This meant they would tell the people of Benin what and with whom they could trade. The oba stopped all trading with them. The British went to Benin to enforce trade by their rules. When they arrived, the Benin army met them. The British were too strong for them. They took the kingdom. Many of the Benin people were killed. The oba was exiled to another country. The culture that had lasted 500 years was gone.

THE LOST KINGDOM: GREAT ZIMBABWE

In the mid-1900s, Rhodesia was struggling. The African country wanted to be free of the British. Finally in 1980, the people fought and won freedom. They took a new name for their country. They called it Zimbabwe.

Zimbabwe is in the southern part of Africa. Studies tell us that it stands in the same place as the great ancient kingdom from which it took its name. The kingdom was called Great Zimbabwe.

Africa

Zimbabwe

Great Zimbabwe was east of the Kalahari Desert. It was between two rivers. One was the Zambezi. The other was the Limpopo. Yet, it did not reach to the shores of the rivers. It was believed to be "in the middle of nowhere."

How did the kingdom begin? Who were its people? These are questions researchers have tried to answer. They have had limited success. What they have learned has come from studies of the kingdom's remains.

Great Zimbabwe began 600 to 1,000 years ago. It stood on the site of a large gold mine. The kingdom could have arisen from the East African gold trade.

Written language was not used in any form at that time. History depended on oral tradition. That means the customs or habits of the people were passed along by word of mouth. Stories were passed along in the same way. Sadly, many details about the kingdom were not passed on in any way. They were lost for all time.

What We Know

Great Zimbabwe was a young kingdom. It was founded in the 1100s. Most of the other kingdoms were thousands of years older.

The people traded along the nearby Limpopo River. They were thought to be the Shona people. The word *Zimbabwe* is a Shona word. It means "house of rock."

Huge plains surrounded the kingdom. The people farmed and herded animals on the land. The people likely raised cattle. They probably planted many different crops. The land allowed them to take care of themselves.

How were the gold mines important? Great Zimbabwe was a very rich kingdom. It had a lot of gold. It traded the gold with cities on the east coast of Africa. The rulers controlled the trade. They collected taxes on it. They grew very powerful.

Exploring the Remains

Three of the kingdom's buildings were discovered. Some walls were as thick as 16 feet. They were 35 feet tall. An amazing thing was how they were put together. Great blocks of

rock were cut. They were put together with nothing added to hold them in place. No cement or glue was used.

The main building of Great Zimbabwe was very famous. It was the best-known stone building in southern Africa. It was made of granite. Granite was the most common rock in the area. The building stretched more than 800 feet. Almost 20,000 people lived within or near it at one time.

At one time, some people argued that ancient Africans could not have built such complex buildings. They were proven wrong. Sadly, those who tried to prove that Africans built the buildings also destroyed many of them.

The Mystery

What happened to Great Zimbabwe? The end of the kingdom was as big a mystery as its beginnings. It was abandoned apparently. The gold trade died away over time. This caused people to leave. The land became less rich for farming. This made it harder to grow good crops. Drought, or lack of rain, also would have hindered farming.

Researchers still look for clues about Great Zimbabwe. They hope to gain a better understanding of the ancient kingdom. For now, it is still a great mystery.

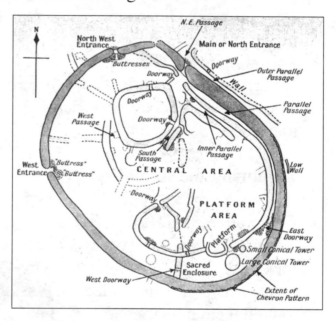

Ancient Africa Speaks

The project was about the rulers of ancient Africa. It was due on Monday. His teacher had said that they were to think of a unique way to present their information. Kofi didn't start until Thursday night. He had a soccer game on Saturday, so he knew he would have to get busy. He would never finish if he waited any longer. Kofi didn't like to sit in the library on a Friday afternoon. His mom had said he could work on his project while she used the Internet to research her new car. So, there he was.

It wasn't that he didn't want to do the report. He did want to do it. He wanted to know more about Africa. After all, Kofi was an African name. His grandfather was from Ghana. Kofi wanted to learn all he could about where his grandfather had been born.

The librarian helped him find books about each ruler on his list. "Well, I guess I'd better get started," Kofi said. He opened the first book and began to read. He read for what seemed to be a long time. He took notes on the information he found about each ruler. As the time slipped by, he became sleepy. His eyelids drooped. Soon, his head landed in the middle of the stack of books. Kofi was fast asleep.

He began to dream. He was in a ship sailing for Africa. Things around him looked different. He could see buildings in the distance. They were not modern buildings of the city where he lived. They were not the buildings he had seen in pictures of modern Africa. It was as if Kofi had slipped back in time.

The dream changed. Kofi was sitting before a large campfire. Many people sat around him. They were dressed in colorful African clothing he had seen in books and magazines. Kofi heard a voice. It was a woman's voice. She was speaking to him.

"Greetings, young Kofi," the voice said. It came from a woman who stood at the edge of the campfire. She was an old woman, yet her eyes shone like those of one much younger. "Welcome to Africa. I am Bisa. You desire to know of the ancient ones who forged the paths for many to follow. Listen to their voices, Kofi. Hear them speak to you." With that, one by one the rulers of ancient Africa began to speak.

I am Taharqa. I once ruled Kush. I was a young man when I became king. I led my armies to fight for Kush. I led them in many battles against our enemies. We battled enemies as far away as Spain.

Much was built throughout my empire. My buildings became legendary. They were many in number. They were majestic. My greatest building was the temple at Sudan. It was carved from the living rock. It was decorated with images of me. Some were more than 100 feet tall.

Many thoughts swirled through Kofi's mind. He had no time to dwell on what he had just heard, though. Another voice began to speak.

*I am Tenkamenin. I was king of ancient Ghana from
1037–1075. My country reached its peak of greatness under my
rule. I controlled the gold trade for my country across the Sahara
Desert into West Africa. My country had riches. It had good
government as well. I helped my people as much as I could.*

*Each day, I rode among them on my horse. I spoke to them.
I listened. I reached out to as many as I could. No one was
denied an audience with me. They remained in my presence
until they were satisfied that justice had been done. My people
supported me. Mine was one of the great models of African
rule. I respected the people and their beliefs.*

"You have heard from two of the greatest, Kofi," said Bisa.
"What have you learned? What wisdom did you take from
their words?"

Kofi thought for a moment. Then, it came to him. "I know,"
he said. "You have to protect the things you are in charge of,
but you can build things, too. That's what I got from the first
guy. From the second, I learned that you have to respect people
and listen to them if you want them to follow you."

"Well said," spoke the old woman. "Listen once more." She
fell silent as another ruler began to speak.

*I am Hannibal. I speak from the land that is north Africa.
I ruled Carthage from 247–183 B.C. Carthage was a north African
country. It is called by another name now. It was my birthplace.*

*I have been called one of the greatest generals of all time. I
used my mind to reach victory and defend my people. I surprised
my opponents. I did things they did not expect me to do. I once
overcame the mighty Alps mountains to reach a battle. We rode
on the backs of elephants into Italy. There we met and defeated
the enemy. We captured parts of Spain. My men and I almost
brought the famous Roman Empire to its knees.*

The voice of Hannibal faded. Bisa looked at Kofi. "Well?"
she inquired.

"That's easy," said Kofi. "You must use your mind to be
successful. Sometimes, you have to do things people don't
think you can or will do."

Bisa smiled at him. "Once again, you have listened well.
There is more."

Kofi smiled back at her. He was proud of himself. The next
voice was a surprise to him. It was that of another woman.

I am Nefertari. I was not a king, but one of the great queens of ancient Africa. I was a Nubian queen. I ruled Egypt with my husband from 1292–1225 B.C. He was King Rameses II. We married to bring peace to Nubia and Egypt. The peace lasted 100 years. We shared power. He built a temple to honor me. It was one of the most beautiful ever built.

When Nefertari stopped speaking, Kofi looked at Bisa. She did not return his gaze. She waited for the next voice. A man's voice was heard.

I, Thutmose III, was pharoah of Egypt from 1504–1450 B.C. I came from one of the greatest African royal families. My sister was allowed to come to power before me. I was angry about that for most of my life. One day, I saw things more clearly. The tasks she gave me helped to prepare me to lead after her. I overcame my anger. I was one of the best-known leaders of Egypt.

Bisa turned to Kofi. "Tell me what you heard this time," she said. "Be quick about it, for the end of your dream draws near."

"I'm not sure, but I think the lady was trying to tell me how I can work for peace," offered Kofi. "The guy learned to see things another way once he got over his anger. It's like being mad was getting in his way. Right?"

Bisa smiled again and stood. She motioned for Kofi to stand as well. The others remained seated and watched. They remained quiet. Bisa said, "I hope you will remember all that you have learned, young one. Take it with you as you leave this dream world. Listen for the voices. Hear them speak as you grow into a young man. Farewell, Kofi."

"Kofi . . . Kofi," his mother said as she shook him awake.

"Which African queen are you?" he asked sleepily.

His mother was confused. "What?" she asked.

Kofi looked around. He saw the librarian and remembered where he was. He knew he had been dreaming. He told his mom all that happened in his dream as he gathered his books and headed for the checkout counter.

As they started for home, Kofi planned his report. He would pass on all that he had heard from the great rulers. He would teach those in his class as Bisa and the others had taught him. He hoped everyone would listen and learn.

THE GREAT ONES

Hello and welcome to another episode of "Who Is That Guy?" I'm your host, Bob Right. Tonight, we go to ancient Africa. There we will meet great rulers of the past. These men were known as mansa. *Mansa* means king of kings or emperor. As we go back into the history of African rulers, we find two that stand out from the rest. Tonight, we will meet those rulers.

I am here with one of the most famous leaders in African history. He is Sundiata. He is a ruler of whom legends are made. Many stories are told of his greatness and power. Tonight, let's hear from the man himself. Please listen as he tells the tale of his life.

Thank you, Mr. Right. Many different tales about me have been passed down over time. I will share my story with you.

I was born the youngest of 12 brothers. My mother was a very quiet person. She was different, so others liked to make fun of her. I was also very different when I was young.

I was sick most of the time. I had a hard time walking. My brothers loved me very much. They took good care of my mother and me. My father was a great warrior who spent much of his time fighting and protecting our land.

Another warrior named Sumanguru wanted to rule all of Ghana. He went from village to village taking everything he wanted. He killed many people. He came to my village one day. My brothers hid my mother. They wanted me to hide as well. When Sumanguru reached our home, he killed all my brothers. He looked at me and laughed. He said that he would leave me be. He thought that I would die anyway.

Later, I found my mother. We went to another village that was farther away. It was a better place for us. I overcame my sickness and began to get stronger. I no longer struggled to walk. I wanted to become a warrior like my father. I wanted to find Sumanguru and stop him from killing anyone else. I decided to do just that.

I became a warrior. I formed an army. We became very powerful. I was ready to find Sumanguru and stop him. Finally, the day I had waited for came. My army found Sumanguru and his men. We destroyed them in the Battle of Kirina. After that, I became mansa. My people loved me because they no longer had to worry about Sumanguru and his men.

As king, I wanted to take care of my people. I worked to improve farming. My soldiers cleared land for crops. Rice, beans, yams, onions, grain, and cotton were planted. I also knew that my country needed more. Trade with other countries would help.

The wars with Sumanguru had stopped the trading with other countries. I had to get the trade going again. I had control of the gold mines in our country. With gold and the salt we mined, the trade began again. My country prospered.

You may hear other stories about me. Some tell of me doing great and supernatural things. Are those true? I will leave you to decide.

Welcome back. Let's meet another famous leader. We already have learned about his grandfather, Sundiata. Now let's meet the man known as Mansa Musa. He was known for his wealth and generous ways. In his time, both learning and the arts grew. Now, let's listen to the man tell us about his life.

Thank you, Mr. Right. My grandfather was Sundiata. I gained my throne from my father. His name was Mansa Uli. He gained the throne from his father, Sundiata. Sundiata was a very brave and wise man. He founded the kingdom of Mali. My father built it up with trade centers. One that many people have heard of was Timbuktu.

When I took the throne, I wanted to keep up the work that my grandfather and father had started. I did not want to let down my family or my people. I encouraged them to keep learning how to work the land. I also made sure they produced things we needed to survive. I supported trade. My empire gained most of its riches by controlling the trade routes that passed through the land. Gold and salt were the main products that were shipped along the routes.

A large army protected my empire. We were attacked many times. Others wanted our gold. My army also protected traders and merchants. They kept them safe during their travels through the empire.

I loved the arts. I encouraged them in my empire. I invited many of the finest artists, poets, and scholars from Africa to live in Timbuktu. This helped to make my empire one of the best in the world.

Mansa Musa, you lived an amazing life! I want to thank you and your grandfather, Sundiata, for joining us on our show tonight and sharing your lives with us. Your roles in ancient African history will never be forgotten.

Well, that's our show for this evening. Thanks for joining us. I hope you have enjoyed this glimpse into the past. I know I have! Join us next week when we will explore some of the mysteries of ancient China. Until next time, I'm Bob Right saying, "Good night!"

THE ROAD TO BUSSA

The following Reader's Theater tells a story set on the edge of an area called the Ashanti kingdom. It is about a foolish civet that traveled to the village of Bussa to get married. The antics of his friends and his own lack of common sense offer a valuable lesson for everyone. One should use common sense even when dealing with friends.

The civet is found in Africa and Asia. It looks like a house cat. It has odor glands like a skunk. The fluid from its glands is used in perfumes.

Narrator 1: Civet Cat was very kind to everyone, especially his friends. But, he was not so wise. He had many lessons to learn. One was about friendship and common sense. This is how it happened.

Narrator 2: Civet Cat was in the town of Bussa one day. While there, he met a beautiful female. He knew at once that he wanted to marry her. He proposed. She accepted. Her father agreed. They set a price as was common at the time.

Civet Cat went back to his own village to gather the things he needed. He found beautiful stones and pieces of bronze. He found copper bars and gold dust.

His bride and her father would be very pleased. He set out to return to Bussa. He was alone. That would not do for a great bridegroom. He needed attendants. He knew just what to do.

Civet Cat: I will stop at the home of Crane. He will travel to Bussa with me. He is my friend. He will be my attendant.

Narrator 1: Civet Cat stopped at the edge of a large pond. He found a patch of reeds. It was Crane's home. He called for Crane. The reeds parted. Crane stuck his head out of his doorway.

Civet Cat: Are you up and about for the day, Crane?

Crane: I certainly am now, friend Civet Cat. What brings you here at this hour? What are those things you're carrying? Where are you going?

Civet Cat: So many questions, my friend, but there is only one answer. I will be married, and you must come along with me. You will be my attendant.

Crane: You are and always have been a good friend, Civet Cat. Of course, I will go to Bussa. I will be your attendant.

Narrator 3: With those words, they were off to Bussa where the beautiful female awaited Civet Cat. Crane flew overhead as Civet Cat skipped along below him. It was just the two of them.

Civet Cat soon stopped again. He picked up a twig and stuck it inside the opening of a small thicket on the ground. Slowly, a dark form began to move inside the thicket like the spread of melted tar. As it came nearer to the opening, its color changed. It took the shape of something long, round, and thick. A head with beady eyes and a forked tongue appeared at the opening. Civet Cat did not run away from it. Crane did not retreat to the treetops. It was their friend, Python.

Civet Cat: Come out, great friend Python.

Python: I am out, Civet Cat. What do you want with me?

Civet Cat: Come all the way out now. I know that there is much more of you than the length I see before me. We are going to Bussa. I will be married there. You must be one of my attendants.

Python: Bussa! Of all the places you might have found a bride, you chose to find her in Bussa. You should have looked closer to home, but you are my friend. I will go with you. Greetings, friend Crane.

Narrator 1:   Crane returned the greeting as Python crawled out of his lair. They were off once again. Civet Cat led the way on the ground with Crane close behind him. Great Python scrunched along behind them. There was one more stop to be made. They came upon a grove of trees. Civet Cat peered in and called.

Civet Cat: Hurry out, friend Rhino. We must be on our way.

Rhino: We, Civet Cat? Why, I have nowhere to go today. What are you going on about?

Civet Cat: We are headed to Bussa. I will be married there. You must be one of my attendants.

Rhino: Why, I absolutely adore weddings, Civet Cat. Of course, I will go to Bussa with you. Greetings, Python and Crane. Good to see you are going along, as well.

Narrator 2: Off went the four friends to Bussa. Civet Cat was pleased with himself. He had found a beautiful female to be his bride. He had his best friends along as his attendants. Nothing could go wrong . . .

Narrator 3: . . . or so he thought. Or, maybe that was the problem, for Civet Cat did not think too well at times. It caused problems for him. This time it caused a big problem. This is what happened.

Narrator 1: After some time, the four friends reached a waterhole. Rhino, Python, and Crane were thirsty. They began to drink at once. Civet Cat did not. He was thirsty, but he thought it improper for a civet to drink straight from a waterhole.

Civet Cat: It is not at all proper for civets, certainly not for one who is about to be married to the most beautiful female in all of Bussa. Wait here, friends. I will go home and return with my own cup. That is the proper thing for me to do.

Python, Crane, and Rhino: As you wish, Civet Cat. We will wait here for your return.

Narrator 2:   Civet Cat went all the way back home. A long time passed before he returned with his cup. He dipped it in the water and drank his fill. Then, they all continued on their way to Bussa.

Narrator 3:   Soon, they came to a nest. It was filled with eggs. They were freshly laid. They belonged to a crocodile that had once befriended Crane. Crane was happy for his friend.

While chatting, they learned that the crocodile was very lonely. She wanted someone to keep her company while she waited for the eggs to hatch. Crane was only too happy to agree.

Crane: Let us stay until the eggs hatch. The crocodile is my friend after all. It would be a pity to leave her when she is so lonely. What do you say, Civet Cat?

Civet Cat: We will wait for you.

Crane: Rhino? Python?

Rhino and Python: Whatever Civet Cat decides is acceptable to us. It's his wedding.

Narrator 1: So, they waited—for 90 days! As soon as the first eggs hatched, the baby crocodiles began to use their teeth. They bit their guests. Rhino thought it best to be on their way after the first bite, but Crane begged to stay until the last of the eggs hatched. They waited. Then, when all the baby crocodiles were hatched, they continued on their way. They were covered with tiny bite marks! Rhino thought it better to be bitten while the crocodiles were young than later when they would be full grown!

Narrator 2: Next, it was Python who caused them to stop. He was hungry and had to feed. They came upon a small antelope. Python caught it and swallowed it whole. The others found the whole matter quite distasteful, but Python was their friend. When he closed his mouth, they started out again. Python did not follow.

Python: Not so fast. I cannot start out again so soon.

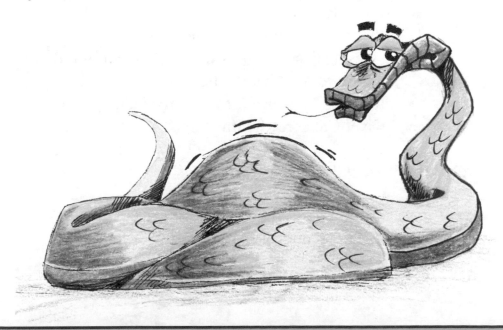

Civet Cat: What do you mean, Python? Have you not satisfied your hunger?

Python: I have, Civet Cat, but after I feed I must take time to let my meal digest. We cannot go. We must wait here.

Civet Cat: We will wait for you.

Python: Crane? Rhino?

Rhino and Crane: Whatever Civet Cat decides is acceptable to us. It's his wedding.

Narrator 3: So, they waited. After many days, the big lump was gone from Python's midsection. He was back to normal and could slither along again. They continued on their way.

Narrator 1: Soon after getting on with their journey, they came upon a forest. It had only just begun to grow. Rhino looked at the young trees. He thought how good it would be to scratch his sides against the trees when he itched. It did not matter to him that the trees were mere saplings. It would be worth it to wait for them to grow. Civet Cat agreed with Rhino.

Civet Cat: We will wait for you.

Narrator 2: Crane and Python were not sure, but Rhino had agreed to wait for them so it had to be as he wished.

Crane and Python:	Whatever Civet Cat decides is acceptable to us. It's his wedding.
Narrator 3:	So, the friends waited—for several years. Then one day, Rhino looked at the trees. He took a good look at them. This is what he said.
Rhino:	Friends, I have been thinking. These are not the sort of trees I first thought them to be. I think they will not be so good for scratching my itches after all. Perhaps we should be on our way. I do absolutely adore weddings.
Narrator 2:	Civet Cat looked at his friends. There was nothing more to be said. They were off again to Bussa. Before too long, they came to a great river. It raged before them. Civet Cat did not think it proper to be wet when he reached his bride, so he said they must stop. They would wait for the river to dry up before crossing it.
Rhino:	But Civet Cat, I can carry you across the river. I will keep you dry.
Civet Cat:	Thank you, Rhino, but I must be sure the river is dry. What if I should fall from your back? It is kind of you to offer to carry me though.
Python and Crane:	Whatever Civet Cat decides is acceptable to us. It's his wedding.
Narrator 3:	The friends sat beside the river. They waited a whole year. That is how long it took the river to dry up completely.

One morning, they walked across the dry riverbed. As soon as they reached the other side, they saw the town of Bussa. They headed straight for the bride's home.

Narrator 1: Civet Cat and his friends had been very foolish. They had tarried too many times on their journey. A surprise awaited them in Bussa.

Narrator 2: Civet Cat found the home of his bride four days later. He knocked on the door. She appeared. She was still beautiful, but she was older. It had been years since they had promised to wed. Civet Cat did not think of this. With joy, he announced himself.

Bride: Ha! You come here after all these years! Look at me! I could not wait forever! I am indeed married, but not to you. I have grown children. Before I close the door in your face, tell me what took you so long anyway!

Civet Cat: Well . . .

Narrator 3: Civet Cat was thinking. He was thinking as hard as he could. Then, he explained . . .

Civet Cat: I went to prepare for our wedding. I gathered my friends, and we started out at once. Then, I had to go back for my cup so that I could have a drink of water. Next, we had to wait for crocodile eggs to hatch. After that, Python was hungry, and it took a long time for his food to digest. Rhino thought some trees we saw would be good for scratching his itches, so we waited for them to grow. Only, they were not the right kind of trees. Finally, I wanted to look my best for you. I wanted to be dry and clean, so we had to wait for the river to dry up before crossing. That took a whole year! But, as soon as it dried, we hurried here straight away.

Narrator 1: The bride could not believe her ears.

Bride: Drinking from a waterhole is good enough for me. It should have been good enough for you. What about crocodile eggs hatching? Who among you is a crocodile? And since when does a mighty python need a baby-sitter? I could have used one years ago! What rhino deals in special trees for his itches? What madness is this? I'll not say a word about the river. It is dried up, just like my youth, just like the promise of our wedding long ago. Go away! Go away, or I'll have my husband take care of you, foolish one!

Narrator 2: At that, the friends heard a terrible growl from within the house. They did not have to think long about what it could mean. Great big Rhino was the first to turn and go. They all ran as fast as they could away from Bussa.

Narrator 3: This time, there was no stopping. The past few days of rain had caused the river to swell with water. This did not stop the friends. The river currents were no match for them.

They came upon the grove of trees where they had waited for Rhino. He ran right over the trees. He smashed a path for the others to follow.

The plains where Python had fed came next. The grazing animals did not run when they saw the friends coming. Instead, they laughed at the funny sight. Civet Cat sprinted. Python stretched and scrunched. Rhino rumbled along. Crane fluttered and flapped behind them.

Narrator 1: The friends made it to the home of the mother crocodile. She waved from a new nest of cracked eggs. Her latest batch of children had just hatched. The friends cast a glance in her direction. They were on the lookout for more biting babies, but they did not slow down at all.

Narrator 2: They finally came to rest at the waterhole. They were tired and thirsty. They felt safe. Surely, the bride's husband had not followed them all that way. Civet Cat stuck his nose into the cool water. He drank until he could drink no more. It did not matter that he had no cup!

THE ASHANTI ADVENTURE

It was time for the annual field trip. Everyone was on the bus. Miss Evans gave final directions to the bus driver. The students couldn't wait to get going. They had never been to a theme park like this one before today. It was the only one of its kind, and it had just opened. They all wanted to ride the virtual ride, Ashanti. Miss Evans had been talking about it for weeks. "The first ride we will take is the Ashanti!" she had said. "Remember to stay together so we can all get on as a group. I want us to enjoy it together."

The bus pulled up to the theme park. Several other buses were there. "Oh no!" said Sam. "What if we can't get on the ride?" Miss Evans assured her that they would be able to ride the Ashanti. She couldn't believe that there would be a problem.

Everyone got off the bus and went through the gate. Miss Evans checked to make sure everyone was there and handed out theme park maps. "Let's go! We will all ride Ashanti first, then you may choose other rides."

They walked to the Ashanti ride and found a long line. "Oh no," they groaned. "What are we going to do?"

"We will wait," said Miss Evans. That is what they did. They stood in line and waited their turn. While they waited, they studied the maps to decide where they would go next. Before long, it was their turn to ride. As they walked in, they were greeted by African drum music. The walls of the room were decorated with African art.

As they found their seats, a man walked through to make sure they were buckled in and ready to go. "The ride goes fast at times," he said. "You will be glad you're buckled in tight when that happens."

Once everyone was seated and buckled in, the lights dimmed. The music became louder, and bright lights began to flash through the room, "Ladies and gentlemen!" a voice boomed. "Welcome to Ashanti! We are so glad you are making the trip to learn about our home. Lean back in your seat and look up. Make sure you hold onto the bar in front of you. Are you ready?" Everyone cheered. They were ready.

"Here we go!" With that, the lights went out. The seats began to move.

"Welcome to Ashanti! You are in for the ride of your life. My name is Rudy, and I will take you through our marvelous kingdom. In our tour today, you will find out where the Ashanti kingdom was and how it got started. You also will learn who its people were and how they lived. Now, let's go to the kingdom itself.

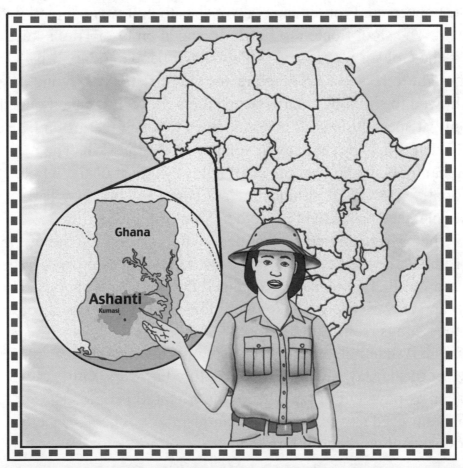

The Ashanti kingdom was formed in what we now know as Ghana. It was in western Africa. The kingdom had a coastline on one border and a forest on the other. The coast made it easy for the British to trade with the kingdom. The Ashanti people made a lot of money. The kingdom grew and became stronger. At one time, it was the largest kingdom in Africa.

The first Ashanti king was Osei Tutu. He set up the government in the kingdom. He made the kingdom strong by taking over the surrounding areas. He wanted all his people to be proud of their nation and work as one.

The famous Golden Stool began with Osei Tutu. A man named Anokye made it. It was said that he had magical powers. One Friday, Anokye called the chiefs of the Union to a great gathering at Kumsai. It was a capital city. At the gathering, the sky became dark, and thunder boomed. A thick cloud of white dust appeared. From it came a wooden stool. It was adorned with gold. The stool floated to Earth. It landed on Osei Tutu's knee.

The Golden Stool is with the Ashanti people today. It is thought to be sacred. There are special rules for it. No one is allowed to sit on it. Guards watch it carefully. It is taken outside only at special times. It is not allowed to touch the ground. The Golden Stool sits on its own stool or an animal skin. The Ashanti people believe the stool holds the spirit of the whole country. They think it holds their strength and bravery. The people have protected the Golden Stool for a long time.

The Ashanti traded a great deal with outsiders. Some of the products they traded were ivory and kola nuts. Gold was traded most of all. The Ashanti exchanged the gold for weapons. The weapons were used to take over more land. They traded for other things from Europe, too.

The Ashanti also traded slaves with Europe and other places. Most of the slaves were people captured in wars. Others were taken as payment of taxes from the captured people. The Ashanti used slaves for more than just trade. The slaves cleared forests and worked on farms.

The Ashanti did not have to trade for food. They could eat crops grown on their land. They could feed all their people.

The Ashanti lived in family groups. Many generations lived together. They were very involved in one another's lives. The families lived in groups of huts set around courtyards. The mothers' clans were the main part of the families.

Sons were trained in skills of their fathers' choices. Boys also were taught to use the talking drums. The drums were used to learn the Ashanti language. They were used to spread news. They also were used in ceremonies.

Mothers taught their daughters skills for taking care of the homes and families. Together they worked in the fields. They brought necessities, such as water, for the group.

The Ashanti people were also master craftsmen. Women spun thread or picked cotton. Men were the only ones who wove threads. Mothers taught daughters to make pottery. Many colors of clay were used. The Ashanti also carved wood and cast shapes in gold.

The Ashanti kingdom remained a great power for many years. Then, it began to lose power. When this happened, the British armies took the land. After many years, it was given back to the Ashanti.

Much of the culture of the Ashanti is the same today as it was long ago. They no longer trade gold and slaves. They are still farmers and master craftsmen.

And now, the tour is over. We hope you enjoyed it. We and the Ashanti people thank you for your interest."

The room went dark, and the ride began to slow. A voice came over the loud speaker: "Please wait until the ride has come to a complete stop and the lights are on before you leave your seats." The class did as the announcer had said.

Miss Evans gave them instructions before dismissing them. "If the rest of the park is a good as the Ashanti ride, we are in for a great time!" she said. The children agreed before taking off to see the rest of the park.

Jungle Jump, Savanna Stomp

Jungle jump, savanna stomp,
Jungle jump, savanna stomp,
Jungle jump, savanna stomp,
Jungle jump, savanna stomp.

Trouble once came to Africa.
The animals began to complain.
You see, they all were concerned about
Too many long days without rain.
They sat around panting in the African heat.
Some tried to keep cool with dust.
"If it doesn't rain, very soon," they said,
"We'll perish. Surely we must."

Then one day, it suddenly happened.
The rain began to fall.
Elephant heard first and lifted his trunk.
He sounded a mighty call.
That was the beginning of a happy dance
They dance to this very day.
I heard of it from an old gray griot.
This is what he had to say.

When Gazelle heard Elephant shout the news,
She darted like a deer gone mad.
Antelope dashed, Hyena yelped,
And Zebra barked, for they were all so glad.
Giraffe looked out across the great wide plain.
Her heart began to wildly pump.
Lion roared out for all to hear,
Saying, "Join in the Savanna Stomp."

The animals danced and whooped and yelped.
They went on like this for quite a while.
It was amazing, yes, quite a sight to see them
Celebrate "Savanna Style!"
Now, listen. Don't think this is all there was
That happened with the animals that day,
For at the edge of the savanna was the jungle world.
There, things were done a different way.

Baboons had been arguing with chimpanzees,
When the first drops hit the ground.
They sat dead still in the tangled treetops.
Prowling Panther stopped to look around.
"What's that he's saying?" hissed long brown Snake.
"Who here can make it plain?"
Warthog grunted with a grin on his face,
And said, "Snake, it has begun to rain!"

Well, that was all it took in the jungle.
Yes, things began to come alive,
For though not quite like the savanna,
The jungle also needed rain to survive.
With chatters, chirps, and grunts they began
To swing, soar, prance, and thump.
But theirs was a different sort of dance.
It was called the Jungle Jump.

Silverback Gorilla waved his arms in the air
And Tiger pawed the jungle floor.
Chimps kept the beat with their clapping,
And the rain really began to pour.
Meanwhile, back on the savanna
Everyone was soaking wet.
Prey danced with predator, friend with foe
For the rain had made them all forget.

After a while, the rainfall ceased.
Back to their homes the animals began to go.
In the jungle and out on the savanna
They had all put on quite a show.
Each one went away, knowing very well
The drought would one day come again.
Then they would dance once more and celebrate
The first drops of the merciful rain.

A Visit to Ancient Africa

The kingdoms of ancient Africa had some things in common. They were quite different from one another, too. Benin is just one example of how the people lived day to day. What do you think daily life in that kingdom was like?

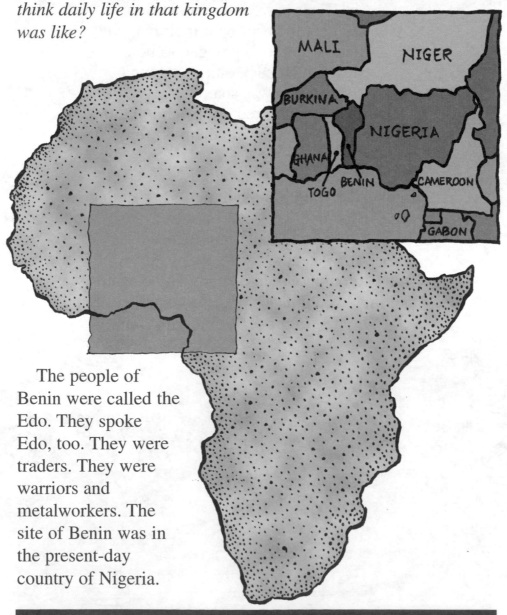

The people of Benin were called the Edo. They spoke Edo, too. They were traders. They were warriors and metalworkers. The site of Benin was in the present-day country of Nigeria.

The Oba

Oba means "lord of the sky." The king of Benin was called the oba. He was very powerful. Everyone had to obey him.

His palace was the most important building in the city. People wore their finest clothes when they visited. It was a sign of respect and honor to the oba. The oba had shrines set inside the palace. They were to honor his ancestors. His shrines were thought to be more special than everyone else's shrines. Many statues of heads were found in the palace. They also were found all around the kingdom. They were models of the heads of people's ancestors. The people believed that the spirits of the bodies lived on in the heads.

An oba often had more than 100 wives. He married to make peace with neighboring kings. All the wives and children lived in a special part of his palace.

Customs and Beliefs

The Benin people worshipped many gods. Osanobua was one. They thought he made the heavens, the earth, and all living things. He had many sons. One son was Olokun, the god of the waters. He was in charge of the sea, the rivers, and the rain. He was most popular with women. He brought riches, health, beauty, and children. Another son was Ogiuwu. He was the god of death. Special altars were set up to pray to him about ancestor's spirits.

The people of Benin believed that there were two worlds. One world was the everyday world. The other world was the world of the spirits. They believed that the two worlds were connected. Things that happened in one world depended on what happened in the other.

The people worshipped the spirits of their ancestors. They made altars for them. The dead ancestors were asked for advice. In the people's minds, the dead spirits would be reborn in new babies. After 14 rebirths, the spirits stayed in the spirit world forever.

The Guilds

Benin was made of parts called wards. Each ward was made of a guild, or group of workers. Benin had about 50 guilds. Each guild lived and worked in its own ward. The guild members were only men. Women were not allowed to join. Boys learned their fathers' skills. When they grew up, they joined the guilds of their fathers.

One guild was for metalworkers. They made everyday things like fishhooks, cooking pots, knives, and tools. They also made weapons. Some men in this group worked with brass. They were highly skilled. They made statues and other things from brass and bronze.

Each guild upheld its own laws and order. They made sure everyone followed the rules. They made sure members were treated with respect. There were strict laws about cheating and stealing. These were not honorable things to do. If someone stole from a visitor, the thief could be put to death. A visitor who stole would be sent out of the kingdom at once.

Travel

Some kingdoms had plenty of horses. That was not true in Benin. It was too hot for the animals to live. The few horses in the kingdom belonged to the oba. They were used mostly for festivals.

Almost everyone in Benin traveled on foot. Because the common people had no horses, there were no carts. There were no carriages. People carried everything they needed in baskets and bowls on the tops of their heads.

Family

For most people, family life was centered on the home or farm. Men took care of the animals on the farm. The boys helped them prepare the land and plant crops. The girls and women tended crops. When it was time to harvest, everyone helped.

There were no schools or books. Children learned how to take care of the home. Their parents taught them.

Women and young girls made pottery. It was an important job. The pottery was used to store water, food, and grain. They made other kinds for drying fish and meat. They made plates and dishes, too. These were considered special. They were kept for important feasts. On ordinary days, the family used wooden plates and cups.

Preparing meals was the job of the women. Girls learned to prepare meals from their mothers. One thing they learned was how to pound grains with a mortar and pestle.

The women ran the markets. People met at the local markets to buy and sell. They found dishes, cups, and firewood there. They obtained woodwork, ironwork, thread, and other items, too. Some foods sold or traded were chickens, vegetables, and mudfish.

Child's Play

The children liked to play just as children do today. They used shells and seeds to play games. They also played with wooden toys.

Storytelling and music were an important part of daily life. When all the work was done, families and friends gathered to tell stories. They also sang songs. Storytelling was more than entertainment for the people of Benin. They didn't have a written language. The storytellers were the historians of Benin. They were called griots. They remembered and retold the ancient legends and myths. These stories were memorized and passed on to other generations.

If you could spend a day in ancient Benin, you would see patterns of work and family life. You also would see people who thought about how they looked and lived. You might see many other things that would remind you of your life. The same is true of the other ancient African kingdoms.

Foods

Poor families did not have many food choices. These families mostly ate the crops and plants they grew themselves. Farmers grew peppers, okra, and coffee. They grew cereal crops like cassava, corn, and sorghum. Grains from these crops were ground and added to boiled water to make porridge. It was the main food of many families. Another important food was yams. A kind of banana called plantains was, too.

Poor people also ate smoked and dried fish. They ate nuts and fruits from the rain forest. The richer families had more foods to choose. They ate many of the same things as the poor families. They ate beef, chicken, or mutton, too.

Water and wine were popular drinks. West Africans did not use grapes to make wine. Instead, they used oil from palm trees.

Festivals

Festivals were important in Benin. They were held for a number of reasons. Some were religious. Others were held for good harvests and a strong empire.

Everyone could be a part of some festivals. Others were held in secret. They were for the oba and a few chosen people.

Yam harvests were special in Benin. Ordinary people could see the oba there. He came with hundreds of men, horses, soldiers, and musicians.

The musicians' instruments were made from simple things. Some were made from gourds. Drums were made from wood and animal skins. The skins were stretched tight across the ends of hollowed pieces of logs. Small, hand-carried pianos were played. They were made by tying wooden strips to a sounding board. Metal was used to make large bells, flutes, and trumpets.

Slaves

As kingdoms fought against one another, they usually took prisoners. Many were kept as slaves. The slaves worked. They gathered firewood and did other simple tasks for their masters. Some slaves served in the army. Later, they could be set free.

In Benin, slaves sometimes were traded for gold. The slaves had many of the same freedoms and rights as Benin citizens. They could own property. They were allowed to marry whom they wished and have their own families. They were allowed time off work to be with their families.

Homes

Most homes in Benin were made of mud. It was shaped and dried. The dried mud made the walls of homes. It sometimes was used to make roofs as well. In its dried form, the mud protected the people from rainfall.

Mud was not the only kind of roof. Some roofs were made with large tree leaves. The leaves were overlapped.

Some homes in Benin were huts. They were made with daga. Daga was a type of cement. It was made by pounding the soil of anthills.

In some of the richer parts of Benin, homes had small courtyards. These courtyards usually were covered with mats. They were cleaned by slaves.

Clothes

The climate in West Africa was very hot. People sometimes wore hats or a kind of sunshade to keep cool. Clothes were brightly colored. The dyes used to color cloth were made from local plants. The clothes were woven from many different sources. Some were made of cotton, bast, raffia, and wool. The male weavers were part of a guild. The women wove clothes in their homes for their families.

The men of Benin wore skirts. The skirts were called kilts. The kilts were decorated with patterns and colors. The women wore long cloths around themselves like dresses. Most of the people did not wear shoes.

Chiefs wore a lot of jewelry around their necks and wrists. This set them apart from the common people. They also wore long robes for special events.

The oba wore very fancy robes when he went out in public. One guild made clothes just for him. His crown had fancy coral beadwork. He wore a high collar necklace. It also was made of coral. The necklace reached from his chin to his shoulders. He sometimes wore another necklace made of leopard teeth. Ivory bracelets and special shirts and skirts finished his outfit.

Body decorations were common. Many Africans wore large gold rings. They wore special bracelets and necklaces. Some scarred their faces. This was done to show their places in the community.

The women's hairstyles were like many seen today. They wore braids and curls. Some women used the oil from palm trees to make their hair shine.

Anansi and Pygmy Hippo

(A poetic folktale of West Africa)

Anansi stories revolve around the trickster spider named Anansi. Akan people of West Africa tell these stories to teach their children life lessons. As with many cultures, storytelling is very important to the Akan people. These stories have been passed down for generations. They were first told long before a written language was developed.

Anansi the spider liked to tend
To his garden plants with care.
One part of a plant had leaves on the top
And another part under the ground.
Anansi said, "I think it is ready."
So he tugged and pulled with strength,
And up from the soil came a yam.
"Yummy!" said hungry Anansi.

"Juicy, sweet yams are really a treat,
And I know just what to do."
Into a pot went the yam with
Butter and brown sugar, too.
He stirred it and stewed it all day.
Out of the window a wonderful smell
Drifted down to the river.

Just as Anansi was settling down
To eat the yam with gusto,
He heard a knocking at the door, and
In walked Pygmy Hippo.
He said, "That yam smells divine!
May I please stay for dinner?
I have surely walked a very long time
Through many trails from the river."

How could Anansi refuse his friend?
He saw that he was drooling,
And the custom in the country
Was to share a meal with visitors.
He put the yam inside a dish
And cut it in two pieces.
Pygmy Hippo was 500 pounds.
Would there be any left for Anansi?

Anansi didn't want his guest
To have any of his tasty yam.
So, he had to think and think
Until he came up with a plan.
Pygmy Hippo removed his jacket
And placed it on his chair.
He sat down with a thud and
Happily reached for the meal.

"Wait!" screamed Anansi aloud.
You can't eat at my table.
You are very dirty, and
You really don't smell very good.
Pygmy Hippo looked at himself
And saw he was caked with mud.
He walked back to the river, and
He scrubbed and scrubbed and scrubbed.

When Pygmy Hippo returned,
Half of the yam was eaten.
He happily reached for the other.
His tummy was really growling.
"Wait!" screamed Anansi again.
"I thought you washed in the river."
Pygmy Hippo looked at himself
And saw he was covered with mud.

Off to the river he went again.
It was late when he finally returned.
The other half of the yam was gone,
And poor Pygmy Hippo had none.
To make matters worse indeed,
He was just as muddy as before.
He apologized profusely
For bringing mud into Anansi's fine home.

As Pygmy Hippo got up to leave,
He looked at Anansi and smiled.
He put on his jacket, and out of his pocket
He took a sparkling diamond.
It looked like nothing Anansi had seen.
"What is that for?" he asked.
Pygmy Hippo replied, "In the dark of night,
It lights my way on the path."

Pygmy Hippo asked Anansi
To come to his house for dinner.
He said, "I want to thank you and
Want to return the favor."
Anansi thought it a good idea.
He had to have that diamond.
He stayed awake for the entire night
Thinking of a way to get it.

The next day, Anansi had a plan.
He thought it was clever for sure.
He spent the morning cooking a yam
Just like he had done before.
He would ask for the diamond, and in return,
He would give Pygmy Hippo the yam.
He put on his finest jacket and
Laughed as he went out the door.

Anansi reached the river at dusk,
And there was Pygmy Hippo.
"I'm so glad you came," he said.
"I have made you a very nice dinner
Of plants, grasses, and leaves I've picked.
I hope it's as good as yours was."
Anansi showed him the yam,
And then he began his trick.

"If you will give me your diamond,
I will give you this sweet, juicy yam."
Pygmy Hippo thought for a moment,
And then he replied with a smile.
"Find my diamond in the river
And then bring it back to me.
I will give it to you with pleasure
And eat that savory yam."

Anansi agreed and thought to himself,
"I really cannot believe my luck.
I never thought it would be this easy
To outsmart my friend once again."
Anansi removed his fine jacket
And gave Pygmy Hippo the yam.
He waded into the river
And looked for the sparkling stone.

When he saw it at the bottom,
Toward the diamond Anansi dove.
The harder he tried to swim to it,
The farther away he would float.
He used all eight legs to paddle,
But that did nothing at all.
He couldn't stay under water;
He was much too light and small.

He climbed on the bank of the river
And took a running leap from there.
Down he went, then up he zoomed
To the surface again and again.
Out on a tree limb, Anansi climbed
And in the river with a belly flop.
Down to the bottom, then zippety zip,
Just like a cork, up he popped.

He finally thought of another idea.
He put on his finest jacket.
He filled the pockets with rocks
And rolled into the river.
Down, down, down he went
And landed right next to the jewel.
"Aha," he thought. "I'll get it now.
I'm such a clever spider."

He tried to lift the diamond
But it was much bigger than he.
With all the rocks in his pockets,
He could hardly move an inch.
He squirmed out of the jacket
And guess what happened next?
He floated straight to the top.
It just wasn't meant to be.

As he crawled slowly out of the river,
Pygmy Hippo was finishing the yam.
And to make matters worse
His finest jacket was gone for good.
He was tired, hungry, and soggy.
Pygmy Hippo said, "Thank you, Anansi,
my friend.
That was such a delicious dinner.
Would you like to visit again soon?"

Anansi learned a lesson that day.
Good things do not come easily.
And trying to outsmart a friend
May lead to being outsmarted.
Do you think Anansi remembered
The lesson he learned that day?
The answer to the question is—
Not a chance and no way!

Nonfiction Note

Pygmy hippos live in parts of West Africa. They are large animals. They get the name *pygmy* because they are much smaller than their cousins, river hippos.

The word *hippopotamus* comes from the Greek word for river horse. Their skin is hairless. It is blackish-brown to purple. Their bodies are shaped like barrels. They have four strong legs and feet. Four toes are on each foot. Their tails are stubby with tassels of yellow hair.

Pygmy hippos can be 40 inches tall. They weigh 350 to 500 pounds. They spend their days resting in shady swamps and rivers. At dusk, they search for food in the underbrush of forests. They eat plants, fruits, leaves, and roots. Their ears and noses have special muscles. These let them spend time underwater. People rarely see the shy mammals.

Pygmy hippos can live 40 years. Most do not survive that long in the wild. Their habitats are being destroyed. Scientists say pygmy hippos are in the vulnerable category. This means they could become endangered in the future.

The African Daily Report

Boy Saves Village From Hunger

Today, the villagers will celebrate the anniversary of a great event in their history. They will remember the day they were saved from hunger. It was not a great hunter who saved them. It was not a great warrior. It was a mere boy. His name was Gano.

His is a story of bravery. It is a story of a kindness repaid. This is how the story is told.

Long ago, the young boy Gano lived with his grandfather, Muto. Gano could not walk very well. He was sickly and weak. Because of this, he was not allowed to hunt with the other

boys and men in the village. Hunting was important. It was important because the people in Gano's village did not know about harvesting grain. They depended on hunting to feed them- selves. Every man had to hunt so that his family would have

food. Since he could not hunt with the others, Gano stayed behind and hunted small insects. He looked for fruits to feed himself and his grandfather, as well.

One day as Gano searched for food, he came upon a wounded bird. Some hunters in the village had chased it, throwing stones. It had escaped, but its wing had been damaged by one of the stones. Gano picked up the bird. He climbed a tree with it cradled in his arm. The men were angry with him for saving the bird. They wanted to eat it, but the boy would not give it up.

Instead, he took the bird home to tend its wounds. He carefully cleaned its wounded wing. He set it straight with two small sticks and some grass. Each day, Gano tended the bird. Each day, the bird grew stronger.

Without realizing it, Gano began talking to the bird. One day, it occurred to him that he could understand what the bird said as it spoke. He asked from where the bird came. The bird simply replied, "Tweety tweet." Though the bird sang the same song each time it opened its beak, Gano understood different things from it.

After a time, food supplies began to run low in the village. The hunters departed to find food. It was a very important hunt.

Days turned into weeks. Weeks turned into months. The hunting party usually returned after a week. The women began to worry as time stretched on without any word from the men.

As time passed, the bird's wing was healed. It was ready to fly. It asked Gano to follow it into the nearby hills. Gano did as the bird asked. At the top of one of the hills, they came to a field of grass. The bird told Gano what to do.

First, Gano picked grass. Then, he smashed the grains from the grass between two rocks. After he did this, Gano mixed water with the grain to form a paste. He added fruit juice to the paste. He made little cakes from the paste and set them in the sun to dry.

Gano tasted the dried cakes. He found that they were good. He knew he would never be hungry again.

As Gano enjoyed the cakes, the bird spoke once more. Gano was to follow him again. Together, they started out on a long journey. Gano was slow. The journey took quite a while.

After several days, they came to a cave. The mouth of the cave was blocked. It was covered with rocks. The bird told Gano to remove all of the rocks that covered the mouth of the cave.

Gano did as the bird said. He removed the rocks. When he did so, he was surprised. Inside the cave, he discovered the missing hunting party. Gano was happy to see them, as they were happy to see him. The hunters told the story of how they had disappeared. They had been tricked into the cave by a strange bird. It had lured them to the cave with its song. As soon as they were inside, the mouth of the cave collapsed. They were trapped.

Gano shared his cakes with the hunters. He shared good news with them, as well. They village need never go hungry again. Gano had found a way to feed the village. He would show the villagers how to harvest grain and make cakes.

As they headed for home, the bird led Gano and the hunters to large fields where the special grass grew. He advised them to move the village there. They agreed.

The village was moved. The people were grateful to Gano. They also were grateful to the bird. They thanked the bird by giving it a place to live. Through Gano, it had taught them to gather and store grains. They would always survive the leaner times. They never had to worry about hunger again.

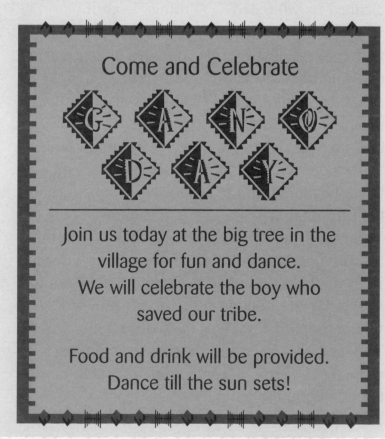

Come and Celebrate

GANO DAY

Join us today at the big tree in the village for fun and dance.
We will celebrate the boy who saved our tribe.

Food and drink will be provided.
Dance till the sun sets!

AFRICAN SNAPSHOTS

Traces of ancient kingdoms may be seen in Africa today. Yet, much has changed since earlier times. Like most cultures, those in Africa changed over time. Some progress further than others. Some change willingly. Change comes quickly to some. It comes slowly to others.

Changes are seen across the continent. Many images are like those in the rest of the world. There are images of war. The country of Somalia has these. There are images of disease and poverty in many places.

Other images of modern Africa show positive changes. Mill workers in Eritrea do their part to build the country. Women, who helped fight for freedom, are now police officers. Some are political leaders. Others are in the military. Night fishermen work off the coast of Gambia.

Shoppers find food and goods at stores in South African townships. Up to 4 million people visit Oshodi Market each day. It is in a big city—Lagos, Nigeria. Many items to buy or sell are there.

Some families start each day by sharing breakfast. They sit at tables in modern homes. The homes are in the suburbs of some large cities. Some children are dressed in uniforms. They hurry to village schools in Angola. Some attend private schools in Malawi. Young men and women train at barber and beauty colleges.

Lights flicker in big cities. Car horns blare. Bicycles weave in and out of traffic. People dine at restaurants.

There is music, art, and dance. It is in churches and homes. Some is traditional. Some music traveled to America. It came back in a new form. It is jazz. It may be heard in the Guguletu Township of Cape Town, South Africa.

These images are snapshots of the great land, Africa. There are many more to see. All testify to the great kingdoms that began there long ago.